PEMBROKE & PEMBROKE DOCK
POSTCARDS OF YESTERYEAR

GW00372872

A eighteenth-century plan of the Milford waterway prepared by Lewis Morris (1701-65).

PEMBROKE & PEMBROKE DOCK

POSTCARDS OF YESTERYEAR

Brian Cripps

First impression—October 1996

ISBN 1 85902 352 5

Printed by
Gomer Press, Llandysul, Ceredigion

ACKNOWLEDGEMENTS

Over the past twelve years or so I have been able to add to my collection of Pembroke & Pembroke Dock postcards, and much of this has been achieved thanks to kind contributions from friends and acquaintances. Postcard dealers and club colleagues at Llanelli have also played their part. However, I am deeply indebted to Kitty Thompson and Arthur Squibbs of Tenby for their invaluable and willing help with details of the photographer Arthur Squibbs (1876-1952), grandfather of the aforementioned Arthur.

I also thank my friend David Hughes of Burry Port for his continued support and interest.

My special thanks, too, to my friend Ray Bowen of Dinas Powis. He has been most generous in allowing me the use of four of his own postcards, numbered 41, 43, 90 and 115 in this collection.

Last, but certainly not least, I thank my dear wife Lorna, who has always helped me to seek out cards at countless postcard fairs over a period of many years. To Lorna I owe this and so much more.

Brian Cripps

FOREWORD

The recent history of the towns of Pembroke and Pembroke Dock is told in this book through pictures. Pembroke Dock can boast over one hundred years of shipbuilding, during which some 260 naval vessels were built, including four royal yachts. The docks area was guarded by a strong military garrison together with the well-known Martello towers, still visible to this day. From 1923 the warship H.M.S. *Warrior* spent 50 years at the Llanion fuel-oil depot as a floating oil-hulk pontoon. It was subsequently 'rescued' from this location and sent to Hartlepool for six years of extensive refurbishment and is now on permanent display at Portsmouth dockyard as the world's first iron-clad warship. In Pembroke the imposing castle dominates the main street, while street names such as Nelson and Trafalgar remind the visitor of the links with naval history.

In this book of picture postcard views I aim to show Pembroke and Pembroke Dock as they appeared to the photographer of the period between 1900 and 1960. The skill of Samuel J. Allen and Arthur Squibbs is particularly evident and is a tribute to their professionalism. Some views will be familiar to many readers whilst others will only be known to but a few enthusiasts.

In 1994 the hobby of postcard collecting celebrated the centenary of picture postcards. During the past 100 years Pembrokeshire cameramen also took the wise step of recording events and views, a selection of which I have chosen from my collection for this latest *Yesteryear* publication. It is a companion to my recent and well received volumes of *Llanelli Postcards of Yesteryear* and *Tenby Postcards of Yesteryear*. Such books are invaluable to anyone making a study of social and local history. Collecting topographical photographic views has now become an important aspect of Deltiology, namely collecting postcards, the world's second most popular hobby.

I sincerely hope that you enjoy the contents of this volume and that you find within its pages as much pleasure as I have experienced in collecting the cards over many years. I hope you will treasure this walk down memory lane.

Brian Cripps.

ARTHUR SQUIBBS
1876-1952

The brothers, Harold and Arthur Squibbs, *c*. 1920.

in 1952. Kitty Thompson (sister of Helen Thompson) had worked there since August 1925 and at the age of 90 years she still lives in Tenby.

Arthur Squibbs with Helen Thompson, who ran the Pembroke Dock Studio until 1941.

Arthur Squibbs and his brother Harold of Bridgewater in Somerset came to South Wales in about 1901 to further their careers in photography.

A studio was opened in George Street, New Quay, on the shores of Cardigan Bay. Some years later Arthur opened additional studios in Charles Street, Milford Haven; Warren Street, Tenby (his principal studio) and also at Water Street in Pembroke Dock.

During the 1914-18 war Arthur was kept busy taking many photographs of military personnel and dockyard installations in Pembroke Dock. The Water Street studio was built in 1921/2 and Helen Thompson worked there from the mid 1920s. From this studio Arthur was appointed the Kodak roll-film agent for South Wales.

During the night of 12 May 1941 the Luftwaffe bombed the Water Street area and incendiary fires destroyed the studio. However, Arthur and Helen survived the war and he finally sold his Tenby studio

Arthur Squibbs' Photo Studio and Shop in Water Street, Pembroke Dock, *c*. 1938. The studio was destroyed by incendiary fires in 1941.

A multiview card showing general views of the Pembroke district, *c.* 1905.

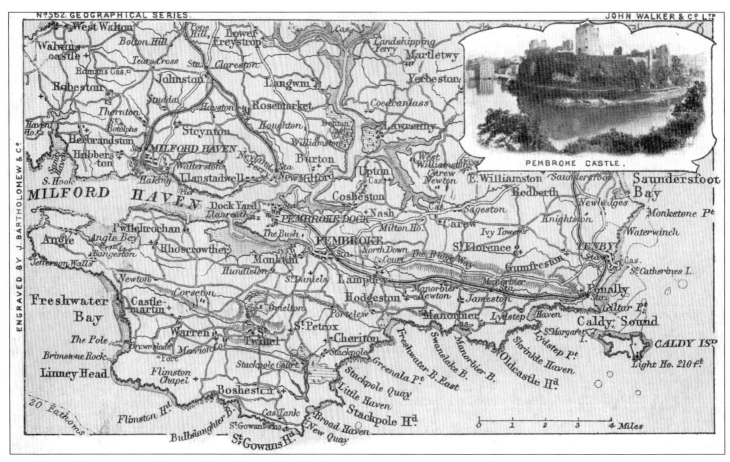

A John Walker postcard map of South Pembrokeshire, *c.* 1912.

A 1903 view of Main Street, Pembroke. St Mary's church stands opposite the Lion Hotel.

A 1910 view of Bush House, home of the wealthy Meyrick family. The house stood on the site of the old Bush farm which was destroyed by fire.

Beyond the parked lorry can be seen William Haggars cinema. Francis Frith published this card in *c.* 1956.

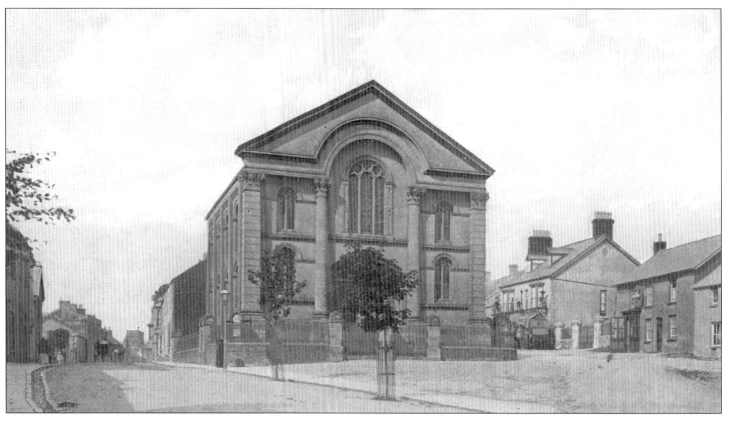

The Wesleyan church in 1910, at the junction of East Back Road and Main Street, Pembroke.

Main Street, Pembroke.

FRITH PBK. 99

Waterloo House, on the left, stands opposite Barclays Bank and the Co-op store in Main Street, *c.* 1955.

A 1909 card of the east end of Main Street clearly shows Orielton Terrace. Can you spot the road sweeper at work?

Pembroke Castle was the seat of the earls of Pembroke for over 300 years. The 80 foot high main tower dominates this view from Westgate Hill, by Arthut Squibbs, *c.* 1936.

A 1914 card, sent from Merlin's Cross, depicting a busy Main Street. A carelessly parked car stands outside the Lion Hotel.

To the right of this elevated view of Main Street can be seen the premises of W. Hancock and sons in Westgate Hill, *c.* 1954.

The mill pond extending upstream of Pembroke Mill. To the right are the outer perimeter walls of Pembroke Castle, and grass tennis courts. The card is dated *c.* 1913.

Afternoon shadows fall across a quiet Main Street and Orielton Terrace. This *c.* 1925 card was published by W. H. Smiths.

Main Street, showing War Memorial and Entrance to Castle, Pembroke

A patient horse with cart stands outside the Lion Hotel, whilst a cyclist adjusts his pedals, *c.* 1920.

An Arthur Squibbs card, dated *c.* 1936, shows a car passing the shop of F. M. Roch.

Bush House, former home of the Meyrick family who in 1813 sold 20 acres of land for the sum of £3,000 to the Admiralty to build the naval dockyard. The house later became a boys' boarding school and subsequently a home for the aged.

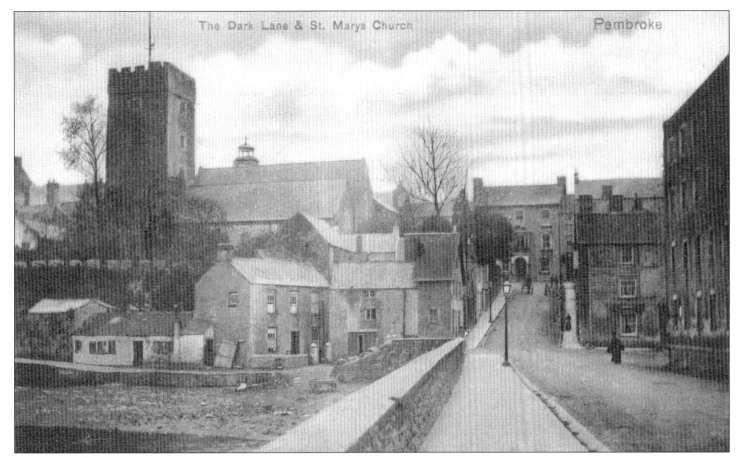

The Dark Lane & St. Marys Church   Pembroke

This card, postmarked 1907, was published by Steward and Woolf. St Mary's church dominates this view from the bridge across the mill pond.

A Valentine Co. postcard of Main Street, *c.* 1911.

Although the card is postmarked 1927, this view of children in Westgate Street, Pembroke, dates from *c.* 1907.

William Haggar's popular cinema, Main Street, 1955. As recently as the 1970s this cinema held a special licence to preview major movies prior to general release.

22035 Pembroke.—Main Street. Church and Old Clock Tower.

Main Street in 1907.

A rare Arthur Squibbs card, dated *c.* 1932, of the atmospheric Wogan cavern under Pembroke Castle.

This view of Pembroke castle and Westgate Hill, leading into town, is by Arthur Squibbs, April 1938.

A brigantine moored at Pembroke quay, *c.* 1908.

Children and men pause to gaze at the cameraman at the site of the West Gateway, 1906.

Pembroke, Dark Lane.

A fine view of Dark Lane and the mill-pond bridge, *c.* 1908.

St Michael's Square and Methodist chapel, Pembroke, 1960.

Children play at the waters edge in this *c*. 1932 card of Pembroke Castle by Arthur Squibbs.

The First World War memorial outside the entrance to Pembroke castle. The card is dated *c.* 1937.

A rare *c.*1907 card featuring the postmistress in the doorway of Hundleton Post Office, by an unknown photographer.

The brig *Mary Jane* moored at Pembroke quay in 1904. This rare card was published by the Excelsior Photo Co.
(*courtesy of Ray Bowen*)

A rare multiview card published in 1914 to celebrate 100 years of Pembroke Dock history.

H.M. DOCKYARD.	VIEW from BARRACK HILL.	H.M.S's "NANKIN" & "STORMCOCK."	VIEW from PROSPECT PLACE.
HUT ENCAMPMENT.	PEMBROKE CASTLE.	CAREW CASTLE.	Sᵗ JOHN'S CHURCH.
MANORBIER CASTLE.	HUNTSMAN'S LEAP.	BULLSLAUGHTER BAY.	STACK ROCKS.

Pembroke-Dock.

A rare multiview card of Pembroke Dock and district by S. J. Allen, postmarked 1923.   (*courtesy of Ray Bowen*)

Albion House is clearly to be seen in this view of Albion Square by Valentine and Co., *c.* 1908.

A view of Pembroke Dock by S. J. Allen, *c.* 1928.

The defended barracks (built 1844-45) in 1917.

An early vignette-type viewcard of dockers in Pembroke Street, Pembroke Dock, *c.* 1903.

St John's parish church at the junction of Church Street and Bush Street, Pembroke Dock.

A distant view of Neyland taken from Front Street, *c.* 1910.

THE KING AND QUEEN LANDING AT PEMBROKE DOCK.

King Edward VII, accompanied by Queen Alexandra and the Princess Victoria, arrived in the royal yacht *Victoria and Albert* in August 1902.

The royal yacht *Victoria and Albert* was built in Pembroke Dock in 1899.

Bush St. Looking West, Pembroke Dock.

A 1911 viewcard showing the old Conservative Club, built 1883, and a superb Oliver's shoe shop, opposite St John's church.

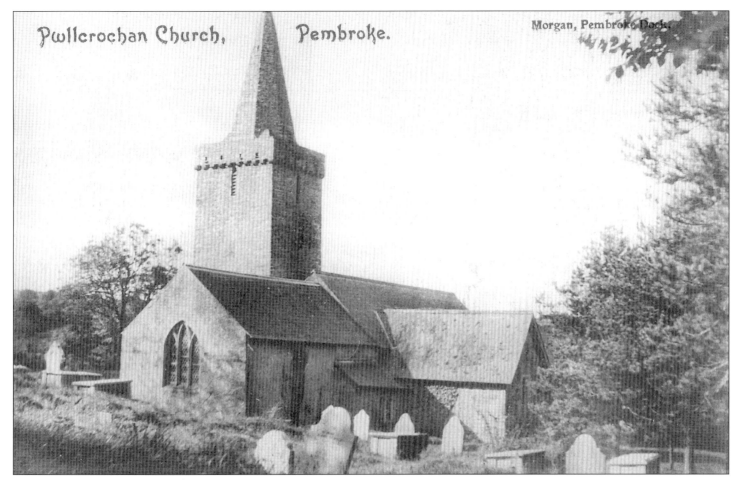

Morgan of Pembroke Dock published this view of Pwllcrochan village church in *c.* 1912.

The white-walled naval wireless telegraphy and semaphore station is clearly visible in this view of Llanreath, Pembroke Dock, *c*. 1906.

The message on the back of this postcard depicting the Vicarage was penned by a soldier stationed at the barracks in 1912.

This 1906 card was sent from HMS *Racehorse* when the vessel was anchored at point X, near the sheds which covered the ship-building slipways at Pembroke Dock.

The bandmaster and regimental goat lead troops of the Welsh Battalion through the streets of Pembroke Dock in August 1912. A visiting warship had filled the town with German sailors.

The covered ship-building slipways, Pembroke Dock. The card was published by Rollings.

The Royal Artillery married quarters, *c.* 1907.

An early 1903 photographic card of dock workers leaving the dockyard via the main gate.

This 1905 card was sent from Colwyn House in Hawkestone Road, Pembroke Dock, 'To the Clockface editor, London'.

A naval destroyer visiting Pembroke Dock, *c.* 1911.

A peaceful Ferry Lane in 1910.

This splendid monument marking 100 years of dockyard activity was unveiled by the mayor Mr W. Robinson on 15 July 1914. The day was declared a local public holiday.

This card, sent from 45 North Street in 1913, shows troops marching from Llanion barracks, built in 1906.

Bush Estates offices, 1909.

Pembroke Dock barracks, 1906.

Children and young people outside St John's church. This S.J. Allen card probably records a harvest thanksgiving event held in *c.* 1910.

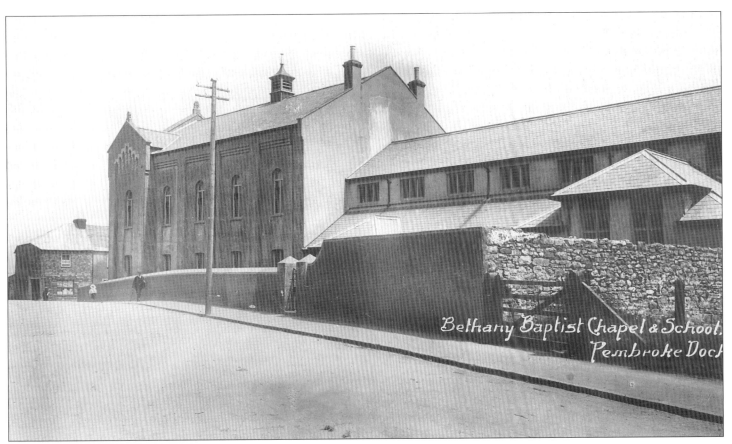

Bethany, the large Baptist chapel at the junction of High Street and Trebowen Road, in 1916.

Bush Camp church and its minister, *c.* 1907.

The two Martello towers in this viewcard were built between 1849 and 1857.

Lipton's grocery store in Bush Street is particularly evident in this card posted on Christmas eve 1905.

Pembroke Dock GWR station taken from Apley Terrace by Morgan the publisher, *c.* 1912.

The Belle View dairy is clearly evident in this 1905 card of Water Street, Pembroke Dock.

Troops queue for a Saturday pay parade within the horse lines of the Royal Engineers in Pembroke Dock, 1911.

A Victorian post-box at the junction of Laws Street and Diamond Street, *c.* 1910.

A Valentine Co. card of Pembroke Dock park.

Three torpedo boats and a destroyer moored off Hobbs Point in December 1910.

Dockyard workers homeward bound, 1913.

The Clarence Inn, in addition to the National School, is shown in this view of Victoria Road, *c.* 1908.

Horse-drawn traffic at the eastern end of Diamond Street, Pembroke Dock.

The Alexandra Vaults at the junction of Water Street and Diamond Street, October 1905.

A police sergeant and constable in discussion at the junction of Bush Street and Gwyther Street (right), Pembroke Dock.

The Pembroke Dockyard Fire Brigade and their fire appliances. This rare card is dated *c*. 1908.

A summer's day in Ferry Lane, *c.* 1912.

A rare view of Victoria Road. A steamroller is in the process of crushing hard core in order to improve the road surface.

An unusual wooden stile alongside the level-crossing gate at Llanion, *c.* 1906.

Coronation day flags fly and pedestrians pause to gaze at the cameraman in this 1911 view of Queen Street.

An attractive vignette viewcard of Diamond Street, Pembroke Dock, in May 1918, published by W. H. Smiths.

Pembroke Dock GWR station, February 1915.   *(courtesy of Ray Bowen)*

A Wykeham series 1904 postcard of the Royal Edinburgh Hotel, Pembroke Dock.

The western half of Pembroke Dock, and Hobbs Point.

The eastern half of Pembroke Dock.

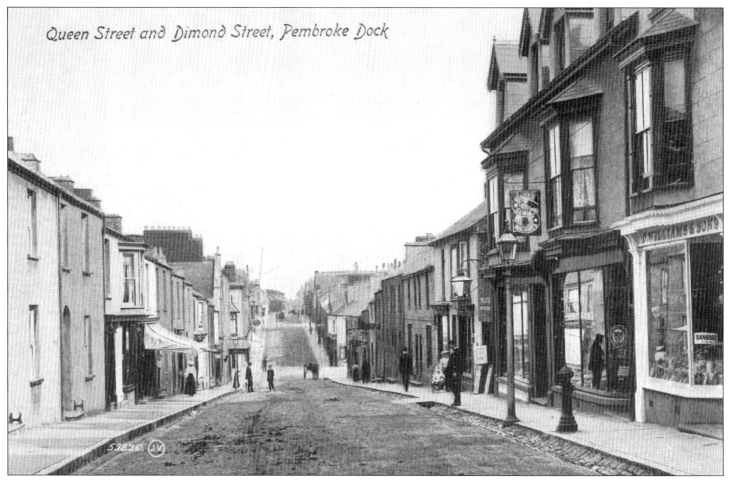

D.W. Williams' greengrocers shop and the Singer shop feature in this view of Diamond Street, postmarked January 1906.

Buffalo Bill's Wild West Show is advertised on billboards to the right of this picture of Pembroke Sreet, postmarked January 1906.

The Clarence Hotel at the junction of Victoria Road and Pembroke Street, Pembroke Dock, *c.* 1912.

A postman pauses outside the Edinburgh Hotel in this early morning view of Queen Street, Pembroke Dock.

The Milford Haven waterway and the covered dockyard slipways used for boat building.

The majority of the houses in this view of Pembroke Dock were occupied by dockyard workers and their families.

VICTORIA ROAD, PEMBROKE DOCK

Pembroke Dock from barracks hill, 1935.

Workers houses in Pembroke Dock, *c.* 1910.

Beyond the town lies Hobbs Point and the oil tanks on the hillside at Llanion, 1939.

A busy Diamond Street, Pembroke Dock, in the late 1950s.

Bush Street, Pembroke Dock, *c.* 1959.

THE FORT, PEMBROKE DOCK.

W.2021.

Five Sunderland flying boats on the Milford Haven waterway. The Valentine card was published *c.* 1954.

Flying boats on the Milford Haven waterway.

An RAF rescue launch, two flying boats and the wireless station near Imble Lane are evident in this 1955 postcard of Pembroke Dock.

A very misleading novelty card of 'Pembroke Dock' published by Valentine and Co. Such cards could be posted for the price of a halfpenny (= 0.21 pence).

A more appropriate Pembroke Dock novelty card. The verse provides instructions as to the whereabouts of the views. This very rare card is by Louis Wain the famous cat artist.

St John's parish church, Pembroke Dock. The card is postmarked 1949.

A rare military card containing mini views of the town. The couplet locates the pictures.

Two young ladies stop and gaze at the photographer in London Road, Pembroke Dock, 1913.

An early view of the naval dockyard, 1904.

A fine group of Salvation Army male musicians in the company of their captain and one lady.

A fine view of Lamphey station, published by Morgan of Pembroke Dock. A very rare card dated 1910.

(courtesy of Ray Bowen)

A LIST OF LOCAL POSTCARD PUBLISHERS

Samuel J. Allen, Bush Street, Pembroke Dock
Wright & Co., 48 Diamond Street, Pembroke Dock
Arthur Squibbs, Water Street, Pembroke Dock
F. H. Phillips, Pembroke Dock
Rollings Stationers, Pembroke Dock
Hughes Printers, Pembroke Dock
Morgan, Pembroke Dock
Hunts, Pembroke Dock
H. Mortimer Allen, Tenby
Excelsior Photo Co. Ltd, Carmarthen

Non Welsh Publishers
Francis Frith, Reigate
Harvey Barton and Sons Ltd, Bristol
Valentine and Sons Ltd, Dundee
Kingsway W. H. Smiths, Nationwide
Stewart and Woolf, London
Davidson Bros, London
E. T. W. Dennis (Dainty Series), Scarborough
R. A. Series, London
Jackson and Son, Grimsby
Judges Ltd, Hastings
William Haddon, Tipton
Milton Carbon Series (Woolstone Bros), London
Hartmann, London
John Walker & Co. (Geographical Series), Edinburgh
Wykeham Collection, London
Zenith Series, Leeds